DRAW
with SIMPLE
SHAPES

by

Jo Moon

ARCTURUS

This edition published in 2019 by Arcturus Publishing Limited
26/27 Bickels Yard, 151–153 Bermondsey Street,
London SE1 3HA

Illustrator: Jo Moon
Author and editor: Penny Worms
Designer: Sarah Fountain

ISBN: 978-1-78950-100-1
CH006935NT
Supplier 29, Date 0419, Print run 7914

Printed in China

Contents

How to Use this Book

Drawing is easy when you break things down into the most basic of shapes. The secret is putting them together in the right way! Look through the book and start sketching whatever grabs you, square by square and oval by oval. Once you've mastered each step-by-step artwork, you can draw it directly into the illustrated scene in this book … and create pictures to be proud of!

Start each picture with step 1, adding new shapes at each step as highlighted.

Create charming scenes by adding anything you have learned to draw.

Here are some of the shapes you will use.
Can you remember their names?

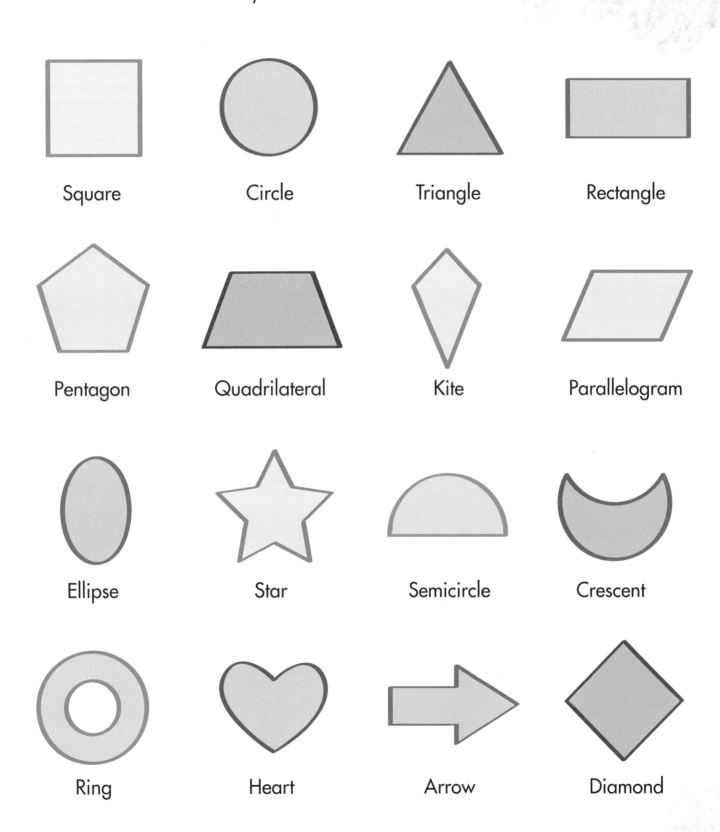

Square

Circle

Triangle

Rectangle

Pentagon

Quadrilateral

Kite

Parallelogram

Ellipse

Star

Semicircle

Crescent

Ring

Heart

Arrow

Diamond

Storybook Characters

Choose a character and bring it to life in the pages of this book. You could draw a knight fighting a dragon or a royal party attended by unicorns and fairies!

Page 16

Page 19

Page 12

Page 14

Page 18

Page 7

Page 8

Page 11

Dragon

Will your dragon be friendly, funny, or fierce? You decide.

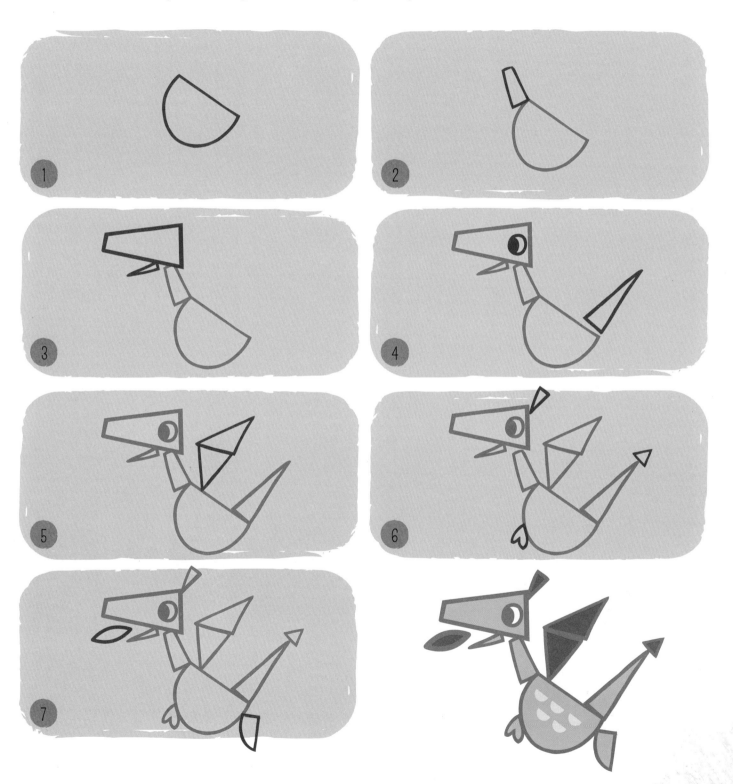

Unicorn

With just a few simple shapes, you can create a magical unicorn!

Fill this enchanted land with friendly unicorns and lots of sparkle.

Add some brave knights to this scene!

Knight

This knight is ready for action and adventure.

Wizard

Abracadabra! Conjure up a wizard using triangles and circles!

Create your own wizarding world!

13

Fairy

Once you have drawn one fairy, draw lots of her friends.

Flower fairies flit and fly through the sunbeams in the sky.

Pirate

Pointy triangles are ideal for sharp swords and pirate peg-legs.

Every pirate dreams of finding a treasure island.

King

King Carruthers is looking for a queen ...

Queen

And, hey presto, you can draw him one! It's Queen Caroline!

This royal couple are holding a garden party. Draw in some friends.

Things That Go

Beep, beep! Chug, chug! Vroom! Whatever noise
these vehicles make, it's time to get them moving.
Don't forget their drivers!

Page 31

Page 30

Page 24

Page 34

Page 26

Page 23

Page 29

Truck

Trucks are mostly made of rectangles. The picture on the side tells you what's inside!

Digger

A digger looks difficult to draw, but follow these eight steps and it's simple!

Every construction site needs lots of diggers!

Train

Electric trains may be fast, but steam trains are awesome!

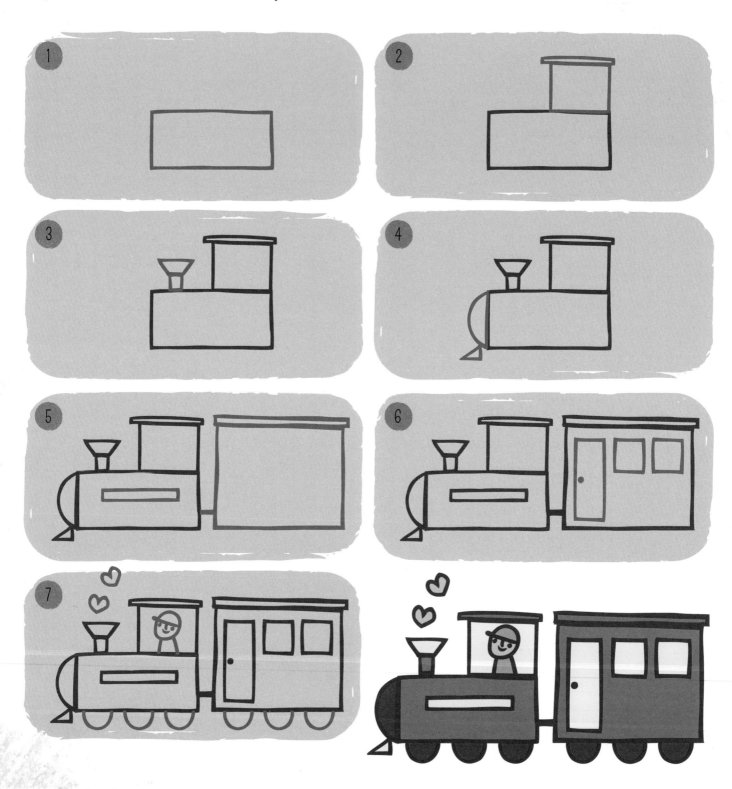

Trains chug to the town and back, along this busy railroad track.

This farmer needs some friends. Bring on the tractors!

Tractor

Want to draw a tractor? A circle is the perfect way to begin.

Biplane

Your biplane needs two sets of wings and a propeller ...

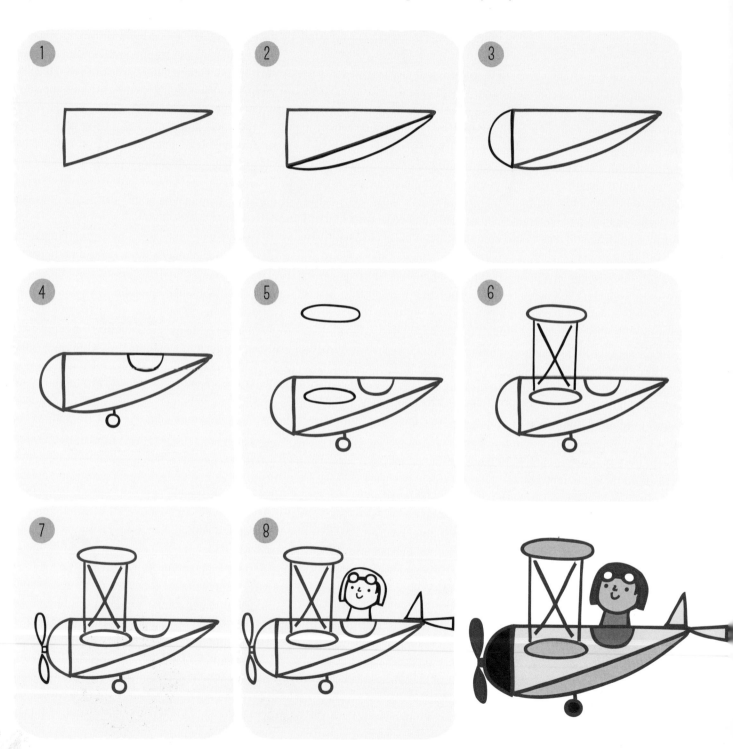

Helicopter

... whereas a helicopter needs rotor blades for liftoff.

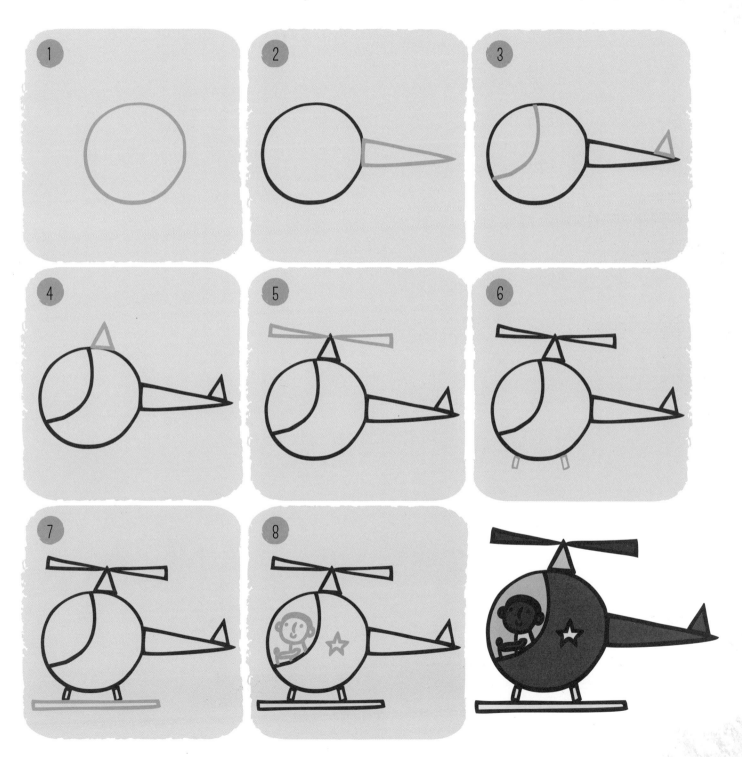

Up, up, and away! Fill the sky with flying machines.

Sailboat

Simple shapes can make simple ships!

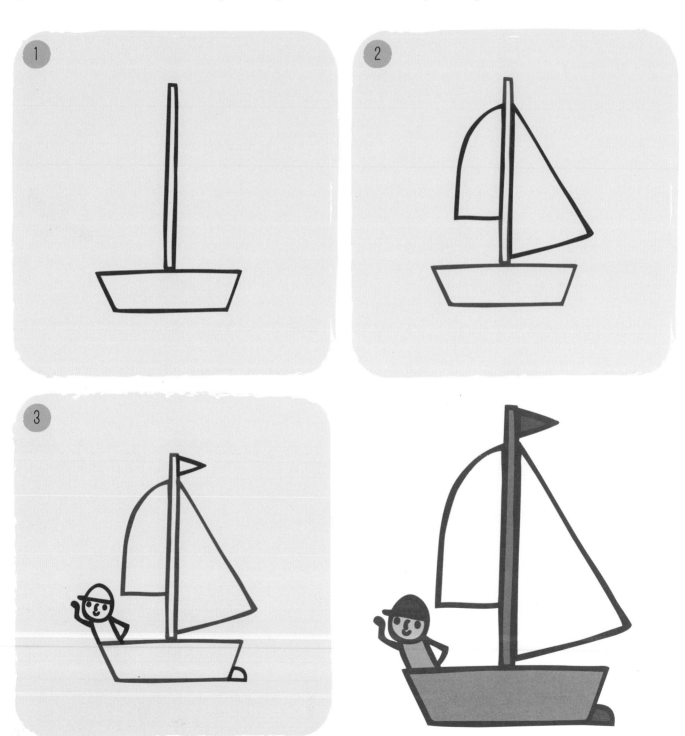

Draw some sailboats having a race. Who will win?

Dinosaurs and Friends

Bring these animals back to life to create
action-packed prehistoric scenes.

Page 43

Page 38

Page 37

Page 44

Page 40

Page 46

Page 47

Pterosaur

Huge, triangular wings help this prehistoric flier take to the skies.

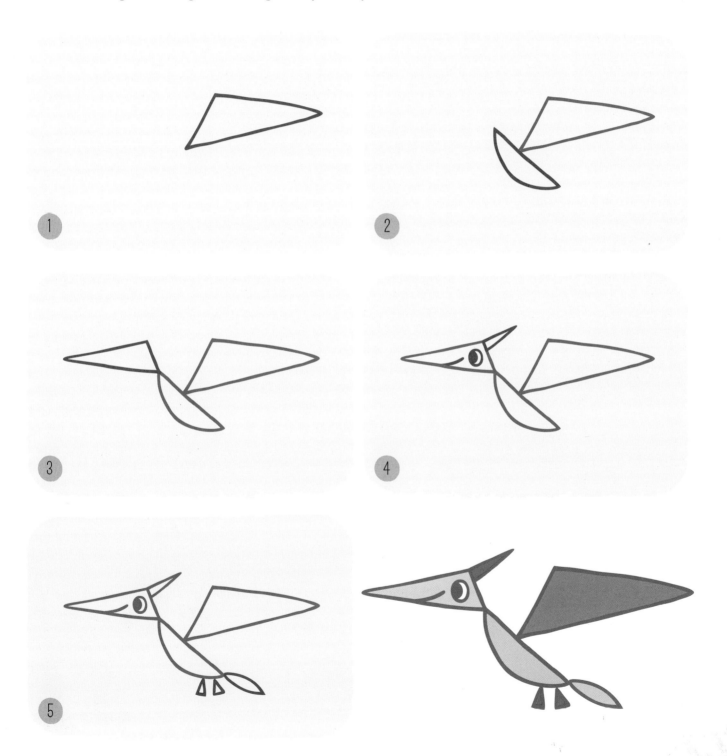

T. Rex

Tyrannosaurus rex is the most famous of the dinosaurs!

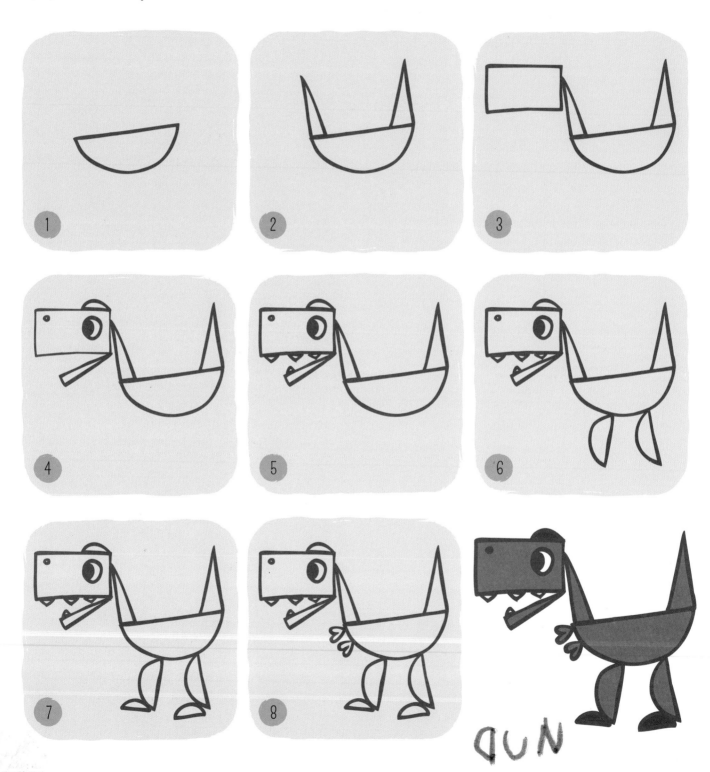

When you draw a dinosaur, make it stomp and hear it roar!

Triceratops

This Triceratops just loves triangles.

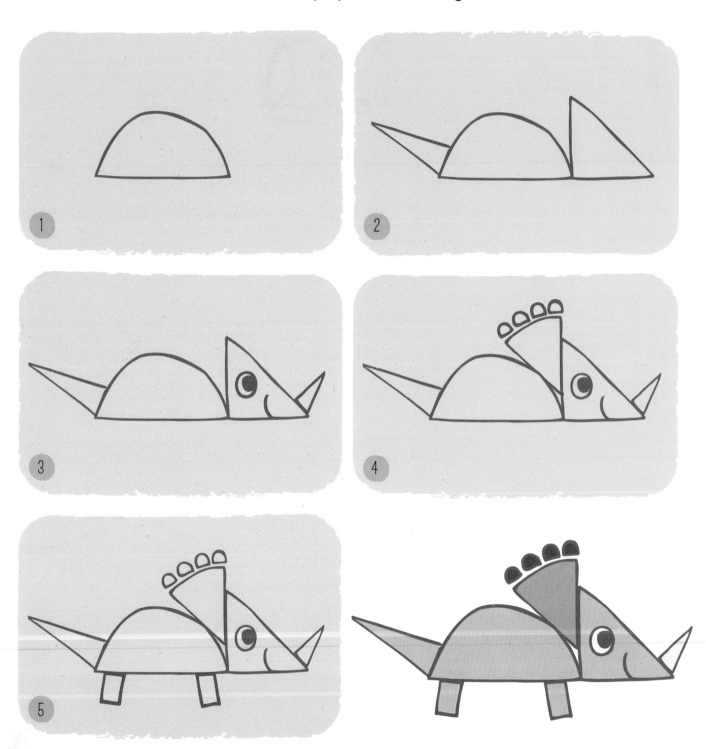

Draw a trio of Triceratops babies.

Draw this little baby Stegosaurus a mama.

42

Stegosaurus

Start with a big round body, and then it's triangles all the way.

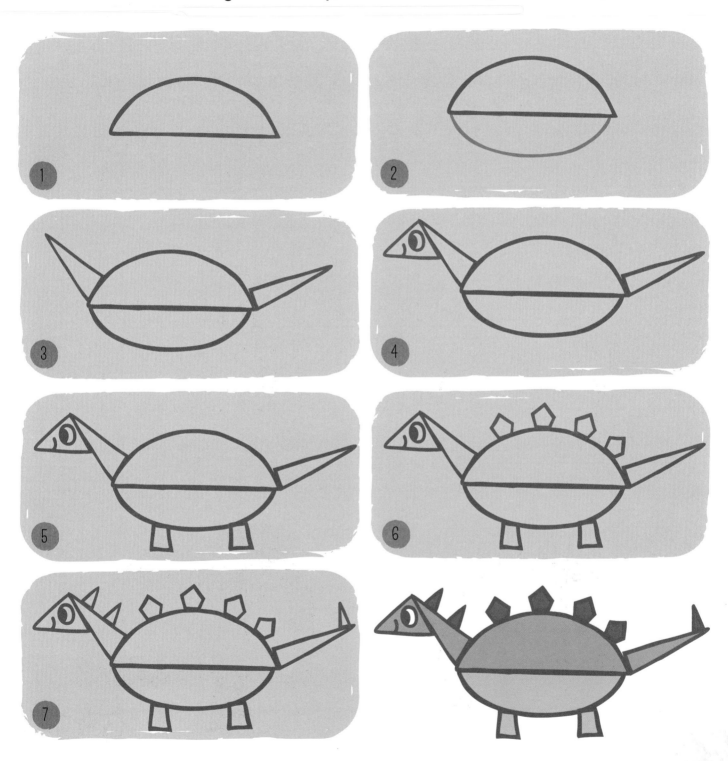

Mammoth

A mammoth was as big as an elephant and as hairy as a bear.

Has anyone seen a woolly mammoth?

Smilodon

This kitty-cat had extra bite!

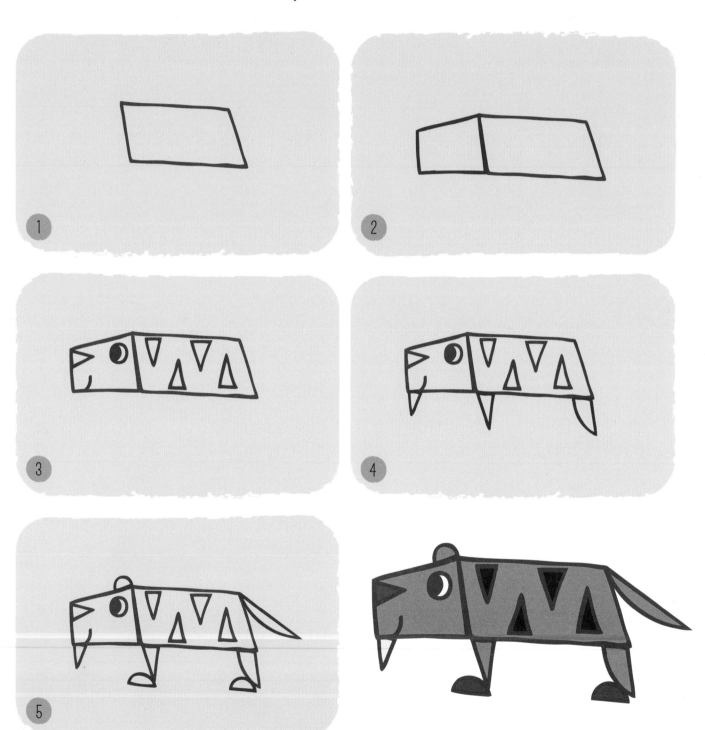

Dodo

What bird had feathers but could not fly? The dear old dodo.

Let's travel through time to create an impossible scene!

In Outer Space

Do you ever look up at the stars and wonder what's out there?
Using simple shapes, you can draw whatever you imagine.

Page 54

Page 56

Page 51

Page 57

Page 65

Page 52

Page 62

Page 60

Rocket

Let's build a rocket to the Moon. 3, 2, 1 … blast off!

Astronaut

Look at this friendly astronaut. One day, this could be you!

Draw the astronaut's crewmates defying gravity.

Flying Saucer

Even an Earthling like you can create amazing alien spacecraft!

Let your imagination run riot.

Robot

This robot has lots of personality. He can even dance!

Robo-dog

Cyril can fetch, sit, and decode alien signals. What a good boy!

Help this factory to build more robots and robo-dogs!

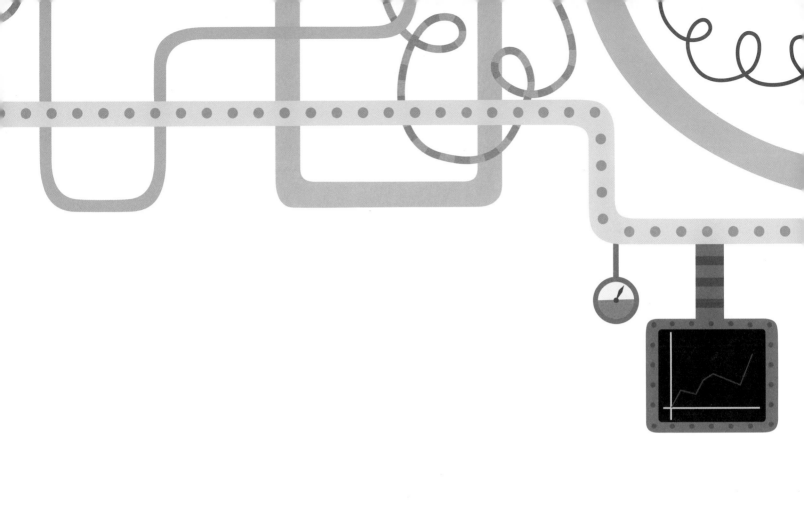

Alien

Have you ever met a friendlier alien?

Draw the alien some friends to play with.

Space Monster

This is Bigfoot's cousin from another galaxy. He's called Bigmouth!

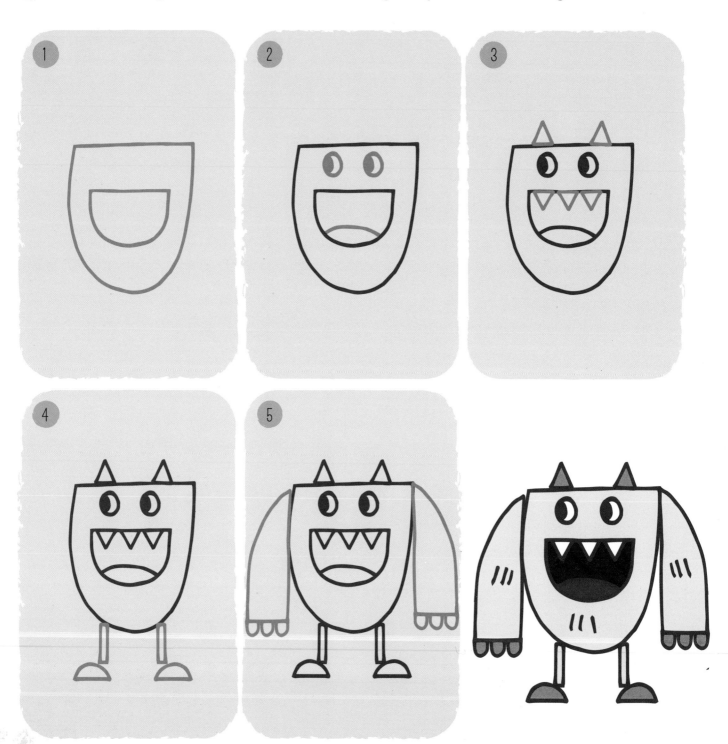

Create monster mayhem in this weird wonderland.

What would you call your own space city?

Space City

Imagine that you're an alien architect. What would your city look like?

About Town

There's so much to see around town, and so much to draw. Add people to your scenes, too!

Page 69

Page 78

Page 80

Page 67

Page 77

Page 70

Page 74

Page 71

House

Once you know how to draw one house, you can draw a whole town.

Who's winning this race at the track?

Race Car

Draw a cool car from simple shapes, and then add your own design.

Scooter

This classic motor scooter can sail past any town traffic.

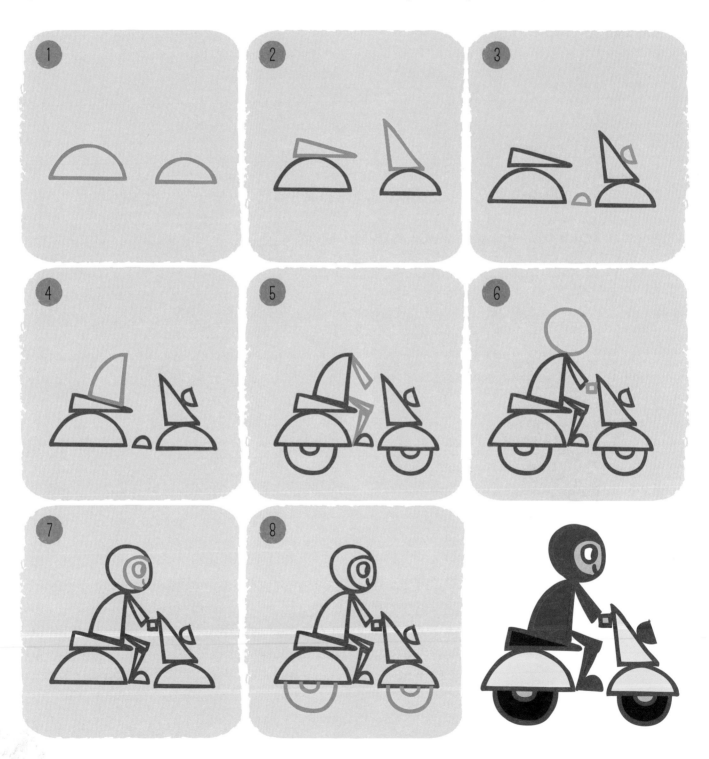

Bus

A bus is a rectangle with wheels and windows—just add people!

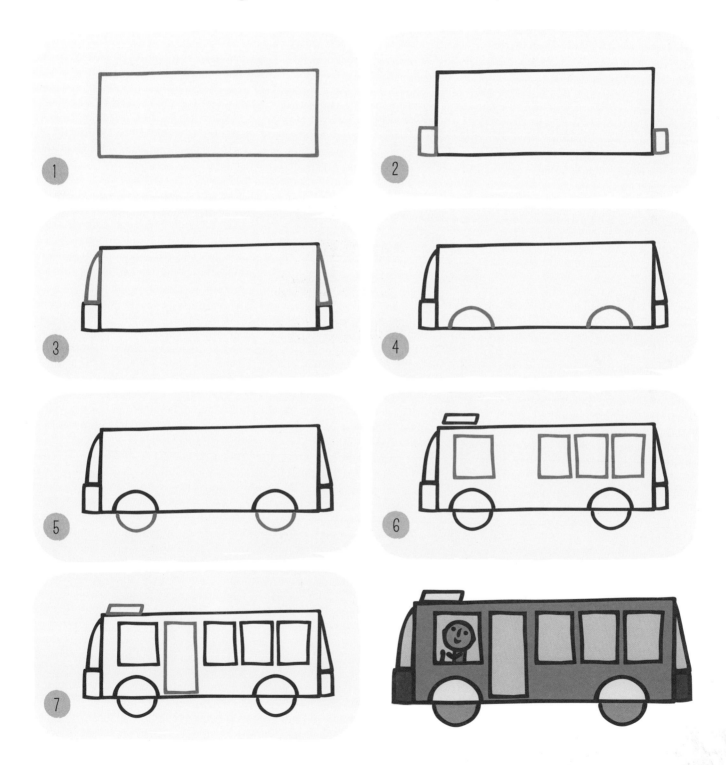

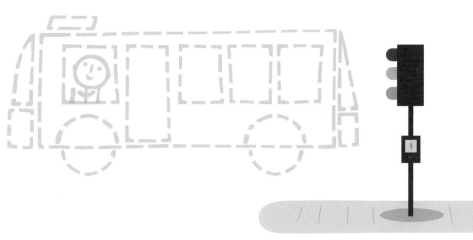

What are these people waiting for?

Clock Tower

Rising above the town, the clock tower keeps everyone on time.

How many clock towers will your town have?

It's playtime at the park. Draw trees for the birds.

Tree

Trees come in all shapes and sizes. Here's an unusual one to draw.

Palace

Create a grand palace with turrets and towers.

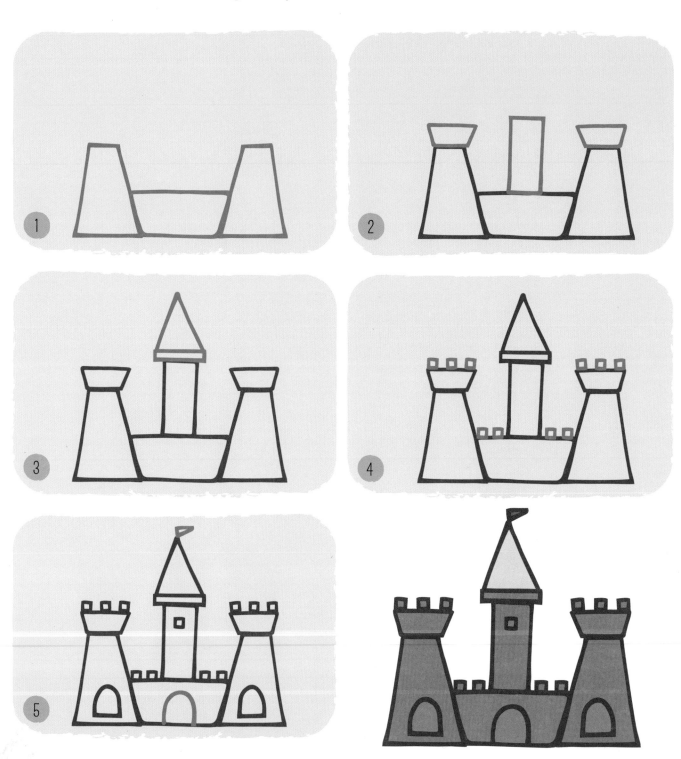

This royal garden is just waiting for some visitors.

Market Stall

Once you've drawn one stall, you can create a whole farmers' market.

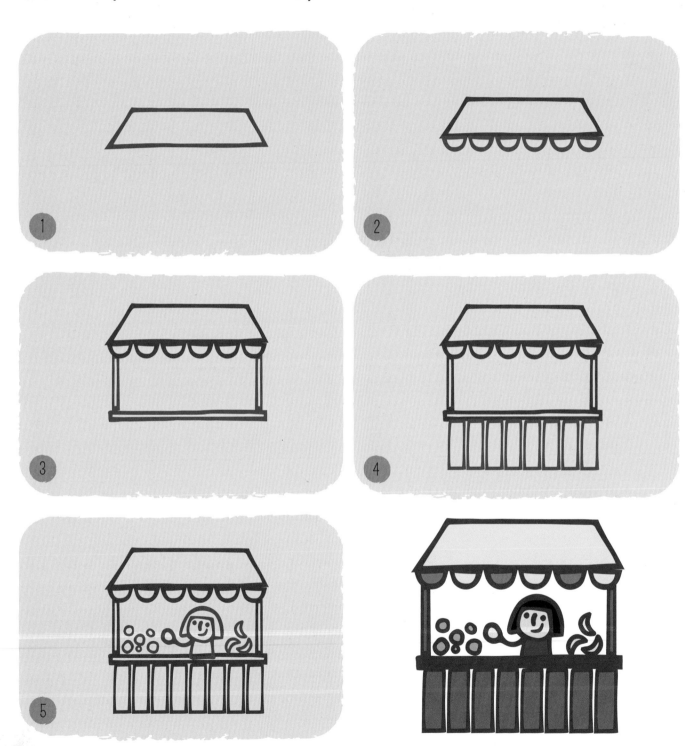

Will your market stall sell bread and cakes, or delicious milkshakes?

Creepy Crawlies

Tiny creatures are fascinating to watch,
and can be even more fun to draw.

Page 88

Page 92

Page 91

Page 93

Page 86

Page 83

Page 85

Cute Bug

To draw your own spotty friend, start with a semicircle and follow the steps.

Draw a group of snails and their slimy trails.

Snail

This snail has big, round eyes and a big, round shell to call home.

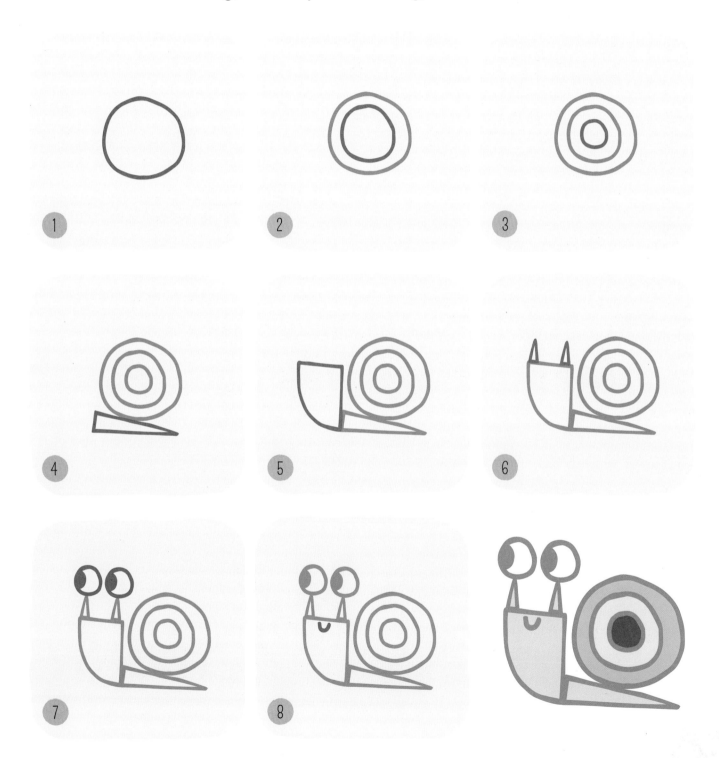

Caterpillar

This cheeky little caterpillar has a lot of legs!

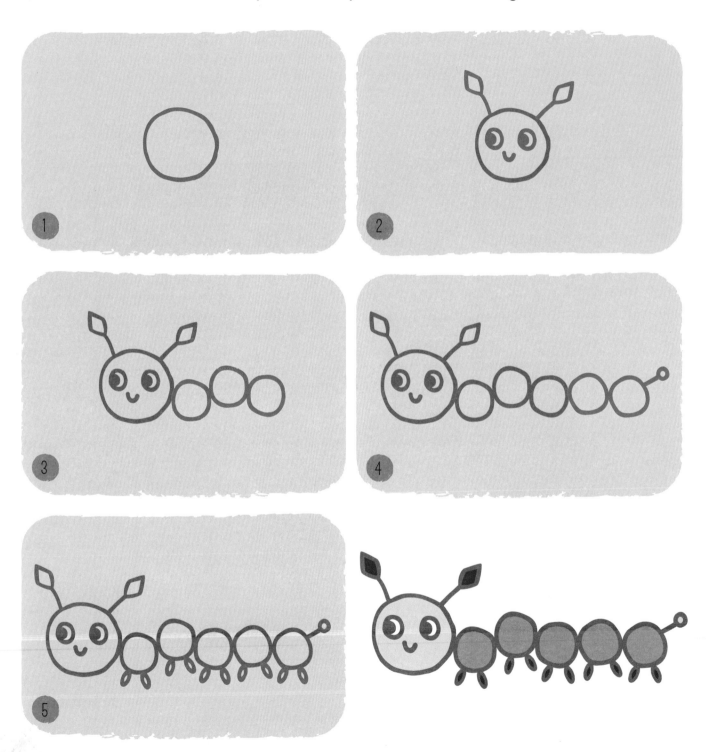

A caterpillar's home is always full of delicious flowers.

Grasshopper

Hop to it and get drawing! Grasshoppers never stay still for long.

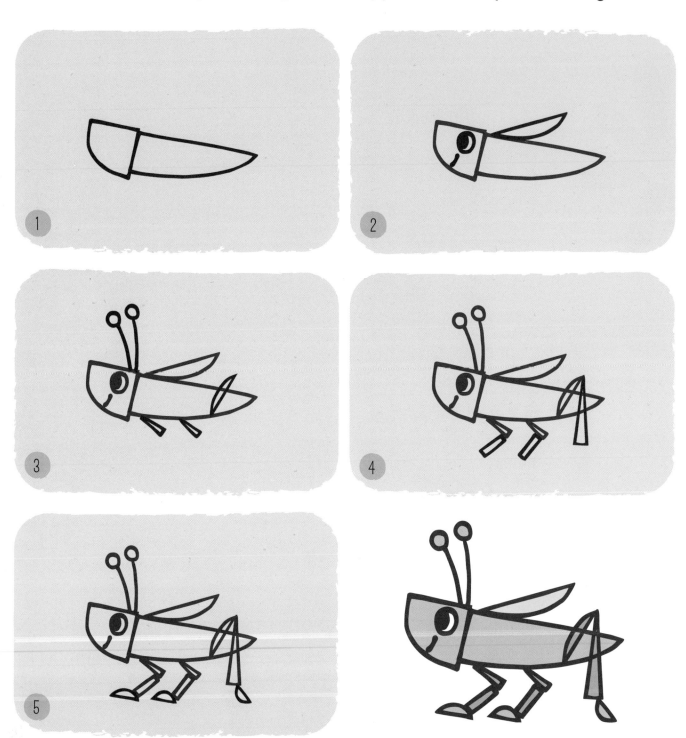

Turn this into a meadow full of grasshoppers.

This mama spider wants a web of baby spiders.

Spider

Make sure you draw all eight legs on this cute spider.

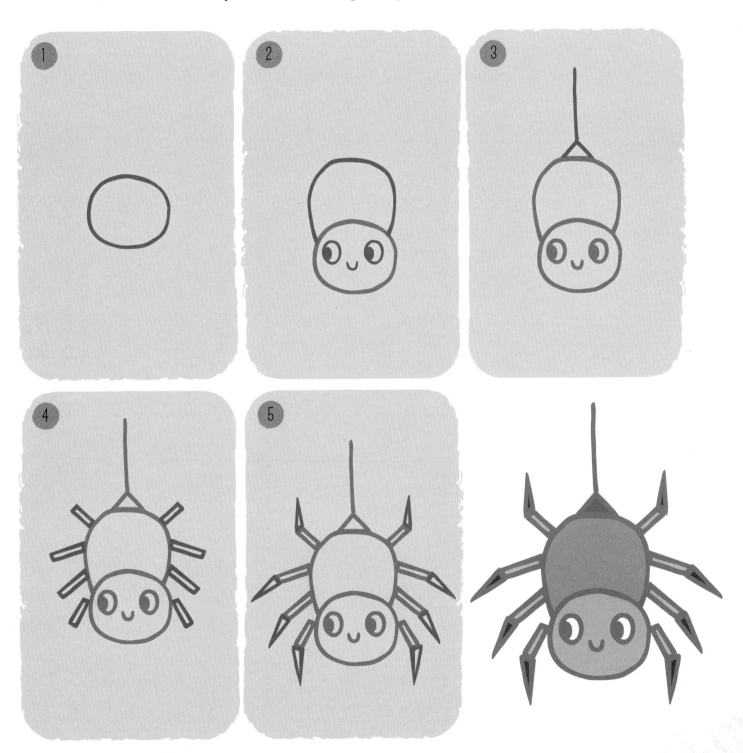

Shield Bug

A shield bug can be green, yellow, orange, blue … or all four!

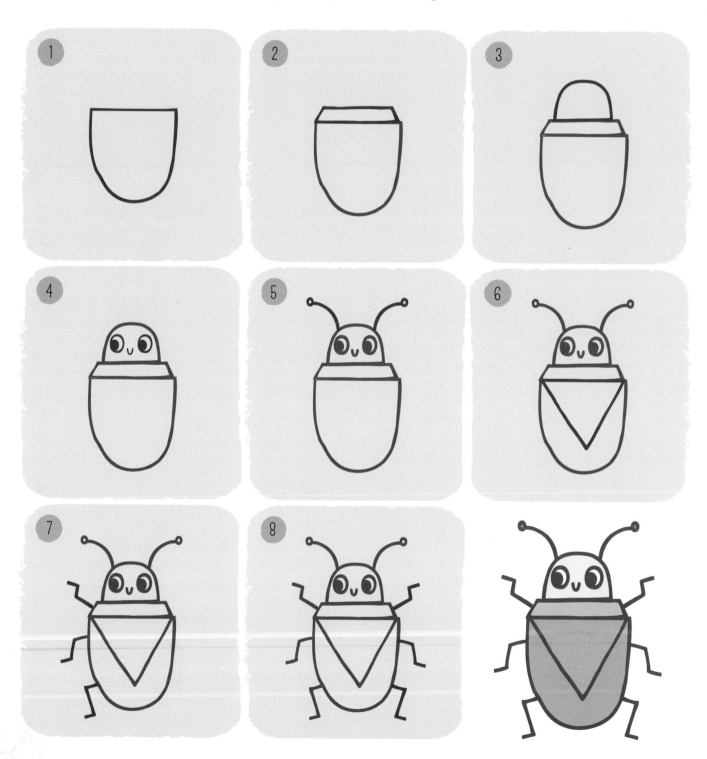

Scorpion

There is no sting in this sweet scorpion's tail.

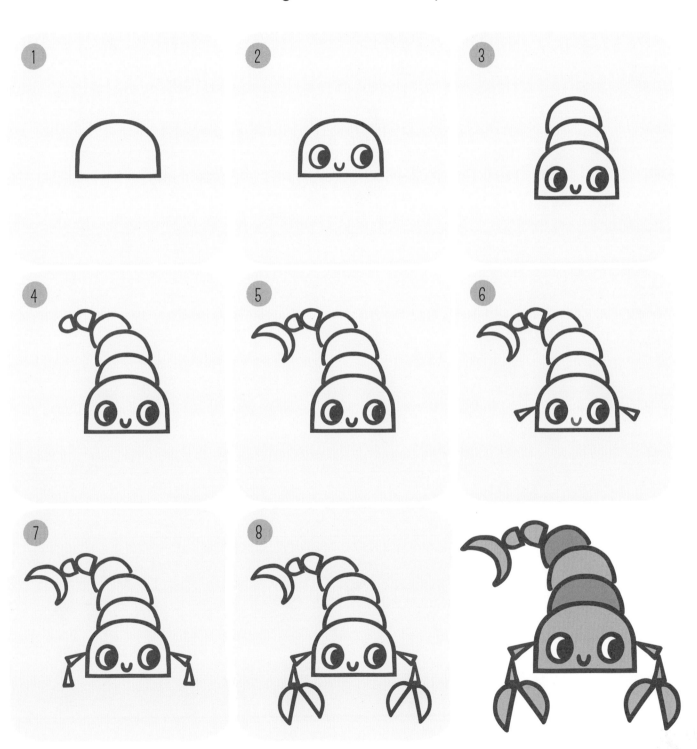

Here is an insect's paradise. Fill it with little creatures!

You've learned to draw so many different things. Which did you like the most? Draw it here!